This book is dedicated to all the children that have been aborted or miscarried.

JESUS SAT ON A STUMP

A Voice for the Voiceless

by Kim Robinson

Book edit and design / *Dorothea LeBlanc*

www.Heavenisfun.com Brightlights-kim@att.net

Photos by *Absfreepic, Unsplashed.com, and Brightlights Photography*

Printed in the United States of America

About the cows on the back cover:

Cows represent birth, motherhood, fertility. Cows sometimes moo when they are looking for their calf.

This book is dedicated to all the
children in Heaven that have been
aborted or miscarried.

"Love is what they do!"

TABLE OF CONTENTS

FORWARD

If you have ever lost a child due to a miscarriage or an abortion and wonder where they are, this book is for you. It's about our children in Heaven.

I understand there are times and seasons when we feel the loss and/or regret of our life's decisions. Other people may not understand the fear that was behind the choices we made but God knows all about what we went through, and why we made our choices.

We can't control what others say or do, and we don't have to try to make them understand. However, we MUST stop looking at the past and instead, look to the future.

God knows us, forgives us, and doesn't condemn us. He loves us deeply and we CAN be free of the enemy's condemnation.

If you have never named the child you lost, the line below is for their name. When you think of them do you imagine them being a boy or a girl? What would their name be, if they were here with you?

_____

_____

_____

INTRODUCTION

The Holy Spirit has been taking me to Heaven since 1988. When I would see Jesus He would show me amazing people, places, and things. We would get to have so much FUN, and I saw lots of children there.

Do you ever wonder where your child is? I can promise you that they are safe in the Father's arms and waiting to see you, play with you, introduce you to their friends, and love on you. But most of all they're waiting to hug you and say, You're a GREAT MOM, You're a GREAT DAD!

Acts 2:19 And I will show wonders in the heaven above... (Parents don't have to wonder where their children are)

Acts 8:39 The Spirit of God suddenly took Philip away... (Philip was translated from one place to another. Translate means to change from one place to another. As the Holy Spirit would take me to Heaven, I would find myself with Jesus, experiencing different places in Heaven.)

1 Kings 18:12 I don't know where the Spirit of the Lord may carry you when I leave you. (The Spirit of the Lord would translate Elijah to different locations for different reasons.)

Exodus 24:9 Moses, Aaron, Nadab, Abihu and 70 elders went up and saw God. (They ate and drank with God.)

JESUS SAT ON A STUMP

On one of my Heavenly visits, Jesus took me to see a place I call "The Body Parts Storehouse," (which I'll explain in more detail later). After we came out of that building, He said, "Do you want to see something else?" I was thinking, "Man, what could beat seeing legs hanging from the rafters?" But I said, "Yes!"

Jesus replied, "Let's walk over here," and we walked up a path. This path, made of the softest tan dirt was on a small incline, deep green grass grew on either side of it. As I walked along barefoot the dirt felt as if I was walking in baby power. I would pick up my feet to look at the dirt and it would fall right off; my feet were always clean.

He said, "Are you ready? Can you handle this?" Again I thought, "Hey, I just handled living body parts hanging from a railing and real eyeballs looking at me," so excitedly I said, "Yes!" Then as Jesus and I kept walking, we approached a large white building. Suddenly a few children who appeared to be around the ages of six to ten years old came running down the path to see Jesus. Three of the children ran up to Jesus and wrapped their arms around Him, laughing, and so happy to see Him.

I thought, "That's how the little children love Jesus in the Bible!" And then one little red-headed girl about 5 years old ran up to me, wrapped her arms around me and looked up at me with a great big smile — and so much love! I looked at her and thought, "Ahh, she's so sweet and loving to me, how nice!" And then the children turned and ran back up the small incline and back inside the building.

As I got closer to that building, I noticed it had a smooth texture on the outside, like smooth pearl or marble, and it had a large white oval-shaped door which appeared to be made of exotic wood or ivory, carved with lots of detail.

Slowly Jesus and I walked up the small dirt incline that led to the oval shaped door and we stopped. Jesus opened the door with his right hand and swung it wide open. He stepped back for me to see inside. I saw a very long and wide room, full of children. The room was large enough so that maybe a hundred children could play there together at once.

I did not go all the way through the door because all the children were involved in a very loud, but fun and happy activity. So I stood back at the threshold peering around the door frame to see what was going on inside. From where I was standing I did see about a hundred children starting from the left to the right ranging from crawling age to about twelve years old.

The room was brightly lit in white light, and I noticed a lady who resembled a nun; she appeared to be wearing a habit and veil, and was cheerfully watching all the children play.

I thought, "Well, of course a nun would be watching over the children in Heaven because that's what they like to do on the earth; they enjoy kids so much!"

It must have been recess time or something. I noticed the children were playing with a huge, brightly colored beach ball: orange, green, red, yellow and blue stripes. They were so happy playing and laughing with each other, jumping with strong legs and hitting the ball with strong arms up in the air from one end of the room to the other. Obviously, it's Heaven, so no one was getting hurt.

I asked Jesus, "What is this place?" Jesus said, "These are the children who have been aborted; they are being raised here with Me."

I thought, "They *know* why they are here... I bet they have so much hatred for their moms and dads, and for the doctors and nurses and everyone else involved."

Jesus turned and looked at me and said, "No, they don't have any hatred for them. They love them all! They know who was really behind it; the devil was the one who caused the lust and inspired the actions. They don't hate anyone. Love is what they do. They love their parents and are not mad at anyone."

Then Jesus slowly closed the door. I could see that He was feeling really sad. I watched as He walked over to a tree stump and sat down. He began to cry — a deep heavy cry from the heart.

Suddenly I was aware of a very, very tall man standing beside me. It was an angel and I asked Him, "Why is Jesus crying like that?" The angel said, "Another one just arrived."

Later that day while I was praying in my home, I saw Jesus standing in front of me in a vision. I asked Him, "Why were you sitting on a tree stump? Why wasn't it a golden throne or chair?"

He said, "What does a stump represent? … It is something that began to grow but was cut off." He also told me at that time, that the little red-haired girl who was about five years old, was mine!

You see, I had an abortion at nineteen, and it never dawned on me that the little red headed girl could possibly be mine… until Jesus told me. All I knew was that she looked up at me with such love. I didn't know who she was, but she knew who I was!

I have named her Joy because she is very much alive, full of joy, and loves me. She has known nothing but Heaven: with no shame, guilt, or hatred.

Matthew 18:11 says, "It is not the will of the Father that one should be lost."

JOY INTRODUCES ME

While I was praying in my home on Earth one day, I saw Jesus in Heaven, and I just walked up to where He was and we hugged, then we sat next to each other but I don't recall what we sat on.

I noticed the tips of His hair as they sparkled, each strand of hair had a star-like light on the ends. His hair went just past His shoulders (which is longer than it normally is when I see Him) and it was so amazingly beautiful as it sparkled with all the starlights. (We have highlights in our hair but Jesus has starlights in His.)

Then He draped his beautiful long starlit hair over me so I was covered in His hair. This made me feel like when I was younger and would play with my girlfriend's long hair or would wear a wig to play dress up. This time spent with Jesus made me feel so loved, like I was and will always be His little girl!

He turned His head to see someone approaching and when I turned, I saw Joy, my daughter, running up to me!

This was one of the first times I got to touch and interact with Joy. This time, she appeared to be in her late teens.

I was definitely nervous not knowing what she was
going to do. But with Jesus sitting and watching I knew
He would intervene if needed. To my great surprise she
yelled out loud so everyone could hear, "Mom you're
here! Look everyone, Mom is here! Mom, I want to
introduce you to all of my friends. Hey everyone this is
my MOM!"

I looked to see the people she was proudly declaring to,
and hundreds of people in Heaven turned to see me!
With big smiles and love they all waved to me, rejoicing
with my daughter Joy. I was feeling quite overwhelmed
that she was so proud to introduce me as her MOM. I
was filled with relief, and then all fear of condemnation
or fear of her rejection left me. My eyes flooded with
tears to know my daughter was proud of me. I had the
biggest smile on my face as she introduced me as her
MOM.

Then I turned back to see Joy's dress. She was wearing a
floor length garment that continuously changed colors.
I turned her around to inspect her and her dress and
saw that even her long hair and her skin were changing
colors too!

She put her hands on my face, combed her fingers
through my hair and said, "Look at you!" I looked down
and suddenly I was now also dressed in a garment that

changed colors. She said, "We match, like mother like daughter. I want to be just like you!" The thought that she would want to be like me was overwhelming for me. I wondered at our color-changing clothes, hair and skin. Then Joy said, "It's because we're close to our Father!"

When I looked up, I noticed that Daddy God, our Father WAS sitting close by, with different colors radiating from Him. He smiled at us. Then Joy looked to our Father and said, "He is so nice!" Jesus walked up to us with His arms out and gave us a big hug, like a group hug and said, "This is My gift to you both; it's each other!"

Before I left, Joy said to me, "Don't worry what others say about you coming here. They don't understand how easy it is to cross over!" We hugged and I yelled, "Merry Christmas" to everyone, and the people waved back towards me.

SOFT FUZZY ANIMALS

Sometimes during prayer or worship, the Holy Spirit takes me to Heaven. One time I felt the Father's love drawing me to Himself, and with the Holy Spirit's assistance, I felt myself step over into God's presence; and suddenly I was in one of Daddy God's blue flower gardens!

God had created a chair just for me, made out of nothing but many different shades of blue flowers. The chair has no frame construction; it's all made out of flowers. The flowers in Heaven are so full of life they are strong enough to hold up a person.

So I walked over and sat in my blue flower chair to watch Daddy God whittling on a piece of wood which He had shown me and told me about on a previous visit: He was making something just for me. He smiled a great big smile and was happy to see that I had come to be with Him and to sit in the chair that He'd made for me.

Then I saw that He had a particular grin, like He knew something was about to happen. I noticed Him turn His head. So I turned to see what He was looking at. A little boy and girl were approaching. They could have been children around the ages of 4 or 5 but they seemed more mature. I guess they might have been small angels. Both had brown hair loosely framed around their faces and they were each wearing a light-colored robe with a tie around the waist; they had no shoes on.

They walked up to me and took me by the hand as they laughed and waved to Daddy God. He smiled and nodded to them as they pulled me away down a green grassy path. They held my hands, as they walked, hopped and laughed along beside me, until we got to a wide and flat river flowing with fresh water. We all stopped next to the river and they turned to wave at someone. I also turned to see who they saw. It was my daughter!

Joy, who at this time seemed to be in her early 20's, was standing beside a white wooden bench with armrests. She stood smiling as she waited for us to arrive. My child/angel guides laughed as they let go of my hands, so pleased in completing their surprise-delivery of me, to Joy. Then they skipped off, running and giggling.

Joy and I hugged and laughed watching the little people skip off, so happy with their assignment completed. Then Joy and I excitedly walked into the water and started playing around, dunking each other, splashing and laughing.

She showed me that there were gemstones sitting on

the bottom of the river, stones of the deepest green, the brightest ruby red, and many other gorgeous colors. We could go under the water and sit on the bottom, still able to talk and laugh, not needing air to breathe. As we sat on the bottom of the river we gathered up the gemstones and I put them into my stomach! In Heaven you just suddenly know things and somehow I knew I could do that.

It seemed so strange that I could place these gemstones in my stomach, but I watched as Joy laughed and did the same. She looked over at me and smiled knowing this was a strange experience for me. As I placed these gemstones in my stomach I remembered from my previous visits to Heaven, that I was a spirit and could easily reach in and out of my spirit.

Later, Joy and I walked a short distance and sat on the edge of a riverbank kicking our feet and splashing in the water so much that we were getting all wet. We actually heard the water droplets sing as we splashed!

When we were finished, a soft white fuzzy animal-like creature flew up to me, it began wrapping, rubbing and rolling all over me, to dry me off. Joy laughed and said, "Oh, they always do that." It was as soft as a chinchilla, but shaped long like a ferret. It flew and I remember how incredibly velvety it felt and how happy it was.

Then Joy said, "I want to show you something". After the fuzzy animal had dried me off, we stood up and turned to walk a short distance over to a huge field filled with green glowing lights. They reminded me of Christmas lights, but they were growing and alive.

We laid down and I made movements, like one would when making snow angels. I scooped some of the lights up so I could carry them in my stomach, like I did the gemstones. I don't know why I put the items in my spirit but once I returned to my prayer room on the earth I felt especially loved, happy and whole. Joy and I ran together playing and chasing each other. Oh, we laughed so much!

I could sense that my visit was ending, so Joy and I hugged each other fully knowing that we would see each other again.

This is not the first time I got to play or speak with Joy; this was the time, however, when I finally knew she didn't judge me for what I had done. I never once sensed any anger or resentment from her.

And now, each time I see her I only feel love and acceptance from her. It feels like we are best friends from long ago and we're picking up just where we left off, full of love and excitement to hear and experience new things together.

Revelation 21:4 He will wipe every tear from their eyes. There will be no more death or mourning or crying or pain. For the old order of things has passed away.

BALL CLING GAME

One day as I was praying, I was taken to Heaven, Jesus met me there just so we could play a game and be together. I had no idea I was going to get to see Joy again.

Suddenly I found myself in a red ball made of a soft sturdy wire-like substance. It looked like a motorcycle cage and the wires seemed to be magnetic on the outside.

The balls were about seven feet in diameter. They were small enough so you could stretch out and press against the sides with your hands and feet (in order to stay stable in the middle) but yet they were big enough so you could run inside them.

Jesus got in a blue ball and I was in a red one. Then we began to run inside our own balls. He laughed and said, "Do you feel like a hamster?" I actually DID feel like how a hamster might feel in a plastic ball, rolling along the floor of a house.

I laughed and wondered how my toes or feet weren't getting stuck through the wires of the cage, but they just weren't. Jesus and I rolled down hills and even across the water, chasing each other, laughing and bumping into each other.

And then, my daughter Joy showed up in her own cage-ball! She reached her arms through the wires to give me a big hug and said, "You're a great MOM!" We hugged and laughed, and then continued to roll around individually in our balls. If I got too close to someone else's ball, our balls would stick to each other, a bit like magnets.

After chasing each other for a while, we eventually all became stuck to one another. Joy in hers, Jesus in His, and me in mine. Our balls seemed stuck together on the outside, but we could still make our balls run along while we were inside, like balls within balls.

One of us would start running and pushing against the inside wall of our ball to change the direction, and the others HAD to follow since they were attached. We ran and rolled inside the balls laughing, not getting dizzy or hurt or tired. It was so much fun!

And then about 10 other people showed up in their own colored balls. We soon clung together to form a huge oblong multi-ball-shape thing: a long molecular design, or just some weird shape that's hard to describe, with all the balls suck together.

When one person would push in a direction, everyone had to roll that way. Everyone was laughing and trying to push hard in order to change the direction. Looking from up above, we probably appeared like a living molecule: rolling, bumping, forming and reforming different designs.

We could stay rolling on the ground or even fly up in the air going in any direction at all. Sometimes we would come apart and then reattach somewhere else in a different configuration.

Father God was watching us playing and laughing and said, "I do love to watch My children play together; I am wise enough to create this game and I am wise enough to fix relationships — even those that aren't fixed yet. Trust Me I know what I am doing!"

My Heavenly Daddy certainly did know what He was doing, I knew what He meant at the time; I knew He was mending relationships on earth, and I have to trust Him and trust in His ability.

2Corinthians 5:8 We are confident, I say, and would prefer to be away from the body and at home with the LORD.

TIME FOR COOKING

One day, after spending some time praying and loving on Jesus, suddenly I was in Heaven — with Jesus standing in front of me!

He was wearing an apron of green and white checked material, and a baker's hat, tilted to the side. He was actually standing behind a counter waiting for me to arrive. I was so surprised that we were in a kitchen together, obviously getting ready to cook something!

I had arrived on the far side of the counter so I quickly walked over to Jesus and we hugged. He had a great big smile and was so happy to spend this special time together with me.

I asked Him, "What are we making?"

Jesus said, "Cookies! Sugar cookies with chocolate chips!" I had never heard of that combination before.

I noticed that Jesus didn't use a recipe. I thought, "Well of course, he made the world, he doesn't need a recipe!" We laughed a lot and talked about how He loves it when His children want to spend time with Him just being together.

As we stood side by side, Jesus and I started stirring the batter in a big bowl with a large wooden-looking spoon, taking turns to stir.

Then I noticed Him look up towards the entryway into the kitchen and smile. I looked, and people started walking into the kitchen through the open entrance. I thought, "He is always available for anyone who wants to come visit".

One of the first people I saw was my daughter, Joy, she was about 20 years old this time. The only other person I recognized was my Mom and she told me to pay close attention to everything Jesus says because He has gold nuggets. Jesus laughed and for the first time I saw my Mom really wholeheartedly laugh.

As Mom waved bye, Joy walked over and gave me a big hug. She was wearing a beautiful dress covered in blue, yellow, and white flowers. (Suddenly, I felt sad because she never had the chance to make cookies with her Mom.)

Then she looked me straight in the eyes and said, "Mom, we are going to have eternity to make cookies and lots of things together!" I could tell she was very excited about the time we'll get to have together — to do all the things daughters and mothers like to do.

She took me by the hand and walked with me around

the kitchen counter; and suddenly we walked into what looked like a huge banquet room!

As Joy and I walked into this large room, we saw hundreds of people carrying and placing food on long decorated tables with white coverings and tons of flowers. Everyone was so happy and smiling, music was filtering through the atmosphere. We stood there looking at everyone, and all the food, and all the flowers, when she waved her arm across in front of her and said, "Mom look at all the joy!"

I thought, "Are there more people here named Joy?" She laughed at my thought and said, "No, not more "Joys" even though there are some here, I mean, there is joy here. And remember, we will have plenty of time for cooking together."

She gave me a big squeeze and kiss and said, "Now I have to go get ready for everyone to arrive!" Joy was so happy as she waved and skipped off towards the banquet tables to help prepare for the arrival of, apparently, a lot of people.

I turned back to Jesus and we finished designing the sugar cookies… and talking about dancing together and letting Him lead. I think this was one of the gold nuggets Mom was telling me to pay attention to when Jesus speaks.

SOMETHING MORE ABOUT HEAVEN AND CHILDREN — A MAN AND HIS SON

This is about a friend, (more of an acquaintance) of mine. His adult son had passed away from an illness about 12 years earlier. Every year on the week of his son's passing, my friend would get very quiet.

One night while praying and talking to Jesus, I remembered this acquaintance of mine, and suddenly the Holy Spirit opened my eyes to see into Heaven. I saw a young man about 20 years old standing approximately 10 feet away from me. I didn't know who he was, we had never met.

The surrounding area or even what he was wearing wasn't the focus, but I remember that he seemed to have on tan clothes, something like a western style shirt and jeans.

This young man walked closer to me; I knew I was seeing into Heaven and was getting ready to meet someone new. I wasn't afraid but curious as he spoke to me and said, "Tell Dad I still have the pocket knife and I'm waiting for him so we can make things together!"

Instantly I knew who he was. Not because he told me his name, but when he said "Tell Dad" I saw a picture of his dad's face flash in front of me.

He smiled at me, waved and walked away to a group of people laughing. I could vaguely see large banquet tables full of food.

A few days later when I got the courage up, I described what I saw to my friend. I had been very nervous to tell him because his religious beliefs were extremely different from mine.

He was surprised, and with tears in his eyes, he told me that his own dad had had a collection of old pocket knives. And one day as his young son was looking through them, his granddad let him pick out and keep one that he really liked.

My friend asked me what the boy I saw looked like, and I described him. He brought out some old photos and asked me to pick out his son. I was kind of shocked but also very relieved when I saw a photo of the young man who I had spoken with in Heaven! The young man in the photo was in his late teens or early 20's (his dad couldn't exactly remember).

Sharing with this father about his son who'd passed away, brought overwhelming comfort and peace to him.

1 Corinthians 15:55 (MSG) Death swallowed by triumphant Life! ....Oh, Death, who's afraid of you now?

KATHY'S DAUGHTER KATIE

One time Daddy God and I were walking on the beach
and He said to me, "You see Me as old and feeble —
like a bent over old man walking with a cane." He
demonstrated how I mentally saw Him at times when I
felt like He wasn't big enough to fix the problems I was
facing. Then suddenly He stood up straight and was as
tall as any mountain you or I have ever seen!

He does not feel or resemble any form of weakness,
anger, or sternness but resembles LOVE, Peace and Joy.

One day after spending time worshiping Jesus, the Holy
Spirit took me to heaven and I was instantly standing on
a sandy beach. I looked up and saw Daddy God. He had
a big smile on His face and held His arms wide open.

This time, He seemed to be about 6 feet tall with big
strong arms and a strong firm body. He was wearing
bohemian style, flowing clothes and a cloth belt around
His waist. He had shoulder length white and brown
curly wavy hair. He looks like Jesus but He is not Jesus,
He is GOD, the Father, who I call "Daddy God".

I ran across the beach and jumped up into His great
big strong arms. He held me and hugged me tight as we

spun in circles on the side of the beach — and the waves calmly rolled in and out.

Daddy God was so happy to just be with me. We spent time walking along the beach, holding hands while enjoying the sand squish under our feet. I was bare foot, but Daddy God wore sandals. (He has big feet! Don't tell Him I said that!)

He asked me, "What do you love about the beach?" I said, "I love those little birds that run along real fast." He laughed and said, "Good, so do I." We continued quietly holding hands while walking on the beach in Heaven.

Then Daddy God started with a thought, that felt to me, like it was right from the middle of a conversation I'd had earlier on the earth with my friend Kathy.

Earlier that week Kathy and I were reminiscing about her 13 year old daughter, Katie (or Kaitlin, as they also called her). She had passed away three years before due to complications from spinal muscular atrophy; which she had when she was born.

Katie had a great love for Jesus and always told of how she could see herself walking, dancing and running with Jesus. She had a great sense of humor and loved to go shopping with her Mom.

So Daddy God picked up on my thoughts without even asking me questions. (He knows every detail of your life. He is full of compassion and really does care about everything that you care about.) As we walked along holding hands, He said to me, "Kim, what I see — you can see!" He reminded me that He is in me and I am in Him (John 17:20-26).

He said, "There are usually two places where you can find Katie. You can find her either swimming with the fish, or teaching the children to worship and dance in the Throne Room!"

We had been walking along the beach, and then the next second we found ourselves standing in the Throne Room! I saw Katie who was holding hands and dancing in a circle with about 25 or maybe 50 kids who appeared to be around the ages of 4-9. They all had banners and streamers.

And then in a flash, Daddy God and I were standing back on the beach as He said, "She loves to swim with the fish. That's her job or position in Heaven; it's to play with the fish — and to make sure that they are played with!"

He said, "She really loves the feel of the big whales, how

they're so slick. She rides on their backs and slides down, then they flip her up in the air off of their tails, as she does somersaults and dives into the water!"

And now we were standing in the air — above the whales — watching Katie slide and flip. When one whale surfaced, she was just flying off the tip and called out, "TELL MOM I'M NOT AFRAID OF DROWNING! I'M NOT AFRAID OF THE WATER! ... WEEEEEEEEEEE!" She did a couple of somersaults and dove back into the water. It was so exciting!

Daddy God and I laughed as we continued to hold hands and stroll along the warm sandy beach, on which we had again reappeared. Heaven is strange but wonderful!

Note that Katie's Mom's response when I told her what I'd seen in Heaven was, "Thank you! I can totally see her lovin' the ocean whales and havin' a blast! I used to worry about her falling off of this floaty that we would put her on. At times when we were in the pool, I'd pick her up in the air and dunk her into the water. I called her 'Free Willy!'"

Acts 2:19 I will show wonders in the heaven above...
(Jesus said to me "they" wonder where their kids are — that is why I am showing you those who have passed away.)

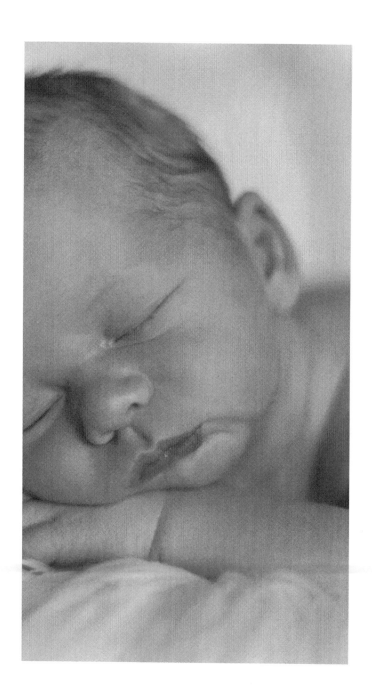

THE BODY PARTS STOREHOUSE — HOPE FOR EVERYONE WHO WANTS A BABY!

One day I was praising, singing, dancing, and worshiping Jesus. Then I quieted myself and focused on Jesus' face. I felt myself walk through into the spirit realm where Jesus met me, and we hugged.

He said, "I want to show you something!" Instantly I was standing on what seemed to be clouds. We walked into a clean white room where legs were hanging from up above, over a rail, like clothes hanging over a railing. They were perfect: they had a knee cap, an ankle, a foot with toes, and flawlessly smooth skin.

I saw spines hanging over a rail with the soft thick cartilage between the joints; they had the neck curvature all the way down to the tail bone, which was perfectly formed to the very tip. There were all different sizes, from infant to adult sizes.

Then I saw various colors of eyes in jars without lids. In Heaven, there would be no need to keep bacteria out because there is no bacteria there. One jar had all blue eyes, one had all brown eyes, or hazel, or green, and so forth. But there are different shades of blues and browns, greens, and hazels, so there were many different jars even for each of the colors. The pupils were perfect, the colors were bright, and even the whites of the eyes were clear and a very pretty white.

After that I saw perfectly formed, healthy lungs of all sizes laying in open trays.

Jesus told me that people whose backs were seriously burned would receive new skin, and people whose faces were burned would receive soft baby-smooth skin. I also knew that anyone who had any type of skin problem was also in this category of being able to receive new skin.

I ALSO saw jars full of sperm on one wall, and jars full of women's eggs on the other wall; there were rows and rows of these. Jesus said, "These are for people who are barren. They don't know how to claim these so they need to find my promises and stand on them."

"Sometimes they cry, plead and beg me for a child; they will adopt, or foster, or volunteer at a school to prove to me what a good parent they would be; they cry out to me to give them children, when all along their children are here! All they have to do is find my promise and stand on it — and they will come!"

For your benefit, I have added a few promise scriptures here for you to stand on. Take time to read and meditate on them.

SPERM AND EGGS

Is anything too hard or too wonderful for the Lord? (Genesis 18:14)

For You did form my inward parts; You did knit me together in my mother's womb. (Psalm 139:13)

Now FAITH is the assurance (the confirmation, the title deed) of the things (we) hope for, being the proof of things (we) do NOT SEE and the conviction of their reality (faith perceiving as real fact what is not revealed to the senses)! (Hebrews 11:1)

LEGS

I will walk before the Lord in the land of the living. (Psalm 116:9)

The blind receive their sight and the lame walk, lepers are cleansed (by healing) and the deaf hear, the dead are raised up and the poor have good news (the Gospel) preached to them. (Matthew 11:5)

EYES

The Lord opens the eyes of the blind, the Lord lifts up those who are bowed down, the Lord loves the [uncompromisingly] righteous (those upright in heart and in right standing with Him). (Psalm 146:8)

LUNGS

God the Lord, it is He Who created the heavens and stretched them forth, He Who spread abroad the earth and that which comes out of it, He Who gives breath to the people on it and spirit to those who walk in it. (Isaiah 42:5)

SKIN

Then [God] is gracious to him and says, Deliver him from going down into the pit [of destruction]; I have found a ransom (a price of redemption, an atonement)! [Then the man's] flesh shall be restored; it becomes fresher and more tender than a child's; he returns to the days of his youth. (Job 33:24–25)

FINAL WORDS

As you finished reading these short events that I experienced in Heaven with Joy and others, I hope it helped you to know that you are greatly LOVED by Jesus and the Father.

Your child in heaven is waiting for you, to love you and spend eternity with you. There is no condemnation or sadness, no hatred or fear of rejection, or shame. If the enemy has been tormenting you with these please let me pray with you:

"Father I thank you for the person who is reading this small booklet today. I ask that YOU Father, right now, would wrap Your great big Daddy-arms around them. Cover them with Your love, draw them closer to You. I command all fear to leave. I command all condemnation, sadness, shame and guilt to leave NOW, in Jesus' name."

Your Heavenly Father loves you. He thinks good things about you. He is proud of you and wants you with Him!

Psalm 139:17-18
How precious are your thoughts to me, O God!
How vast is the sum of them!
If I could count them, they would outnumber the sand.
When I awake, I am still with You.

RAISED BY THE KING

(a poem from an unborn child, written for its mother)

The King watched over me as I was being made. He smiled and held me in His arms when I arrived, I was not afraid.

He placed my tiny hands in His, kissing my nose, my eyes, lips and finger tips.

He clothed me in the finest and gave the best gifts of all. The angels taught me how to fly, how to throw and catch a ball.

Jesus told me stories about you and me. Times we will get to play, go on picnics, have parties, splash in the river that flows under the King.

Jesus carried me on His shoulders, even gave piggy-back rides and laughs when I sing.

He told me of His love for you, and a chair by His side. We pray for you, rejoice with you, don't worry about a thing.

I'm here with the King waiting for you. I'll be standing by the swing.

— Forever your child

 The Holy Spirit has been taking Kim to Heaven since 1988. Jesus shows her amazing people, places and things, and she sees lots of children there.

Kim leads Sozo Ministry; healing hearts is her passion. She has written several books about her experiences in Heaven:

1. *Heaven is Real and Fun* (Experiences Kim had in Heaven)

2. *How to Access Jesus in the Heavenly Realm Manual* (How you too can experience these things)

3. *Jesus is Real and Fun* (A children's activity coloring book about Heaven)

4. *Jesus Sat on a Stump* (A book dedicated to all the children that have been aborted or miscarried)

5. *Fuzzy Bunny and Smiling Monkey* (A children's bedtime story told to Kim by Jesus)

Please "Like" us on Facebook: Heaven is Real and Fun

You can order Kim's books at her website: www.heavenisfun.com

Made in the USA
Columbia, SC
28 July 2024

39573036R00036